Take and Receive

Take and Receive

Poems by

Joyce Wilson

Kelsay Books

Cover design: Shay Culligan

Cover art: Zinnias and Marigolds, 1933, from an oil on canvas by
Hermann Dudley Murphy, 1867–1945, Museum of Fine Arts,
Boston, The Hayden Collection.

ISBN: 978-1-950462-00-1

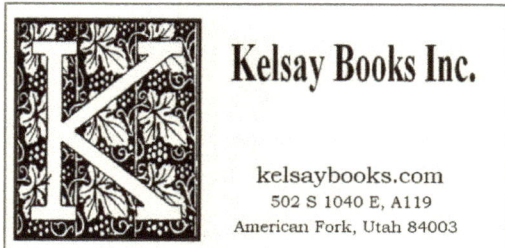

Kelsay Books Inc.

kelsaybooks.com
502 S 1040 E, A119
American Fork, Utah 84003

To my mother Nancy
and my mother-in-law Frances,
in their memory

Acknowledgments

Poems appeared in the following literary journals, some in slightly different form, under different titles:

Alabama Literary Review: "The Speckled Hawk"
Literary Matters of ALSCW: "The Citadel"
Angle: "She Regards Michelangelo's Piéta"
Constellations: "The Fledgling"
Free Inquiry: "Encounter with His Brother"
Grey Sparrow: "Detour," "Like Emerson," "On the Terrace,"
    and "These Cairo Girls"
Ibbetson Street: "Her Tattoo" (#13); "The White Cat"
    "Poisonous Fruit" (#29); "Driving through Amish Country,"
    "Tomatoes in September" (#30); "He Would Not Stay" (#37);
    "The Envy of the Gods" (#39); "Her Passing" (#40); "Late
    Spring at Sixty" (#41)
The Lyric: "Your Coat"
Mezzo Cammin: "My Last Visit," "Take and Receive" (Vol. 2/2); "If
    I Should Leave You" (Vol. 5/2); "My Mother and the Rugosa,"
    "Zinnias and Marigolds" (Vol. 6/1); "Building and Rebuilding,"
    "Privacy of Dreams," "Between Regimes," "Evening into Day"
    (Vol. 10/2); "Kitchen Cleanup," "Family Talk" (Vol. 13/2)
Poetry Ireland: "I Freed a Dove Today"
The Poetry Porch: "Commencement," "Wingèd Creature," "Still the
    Same"
The Sonnet Scroll of *The Poetry Porch:* "Sonnets for Sunflowers,"
    "A Community Gathered" (as "Fire Alarm Tripped"),
    "Unemployed," "On Opening a Book of Poems by Michael
    Drayton…," "Two Temperaments"
Poetry Salzburg: "For the Love of a Book"
Salamander: "Girl in Blue" (#17/1); "Google the Girl," "Bluze"
    (#41); "Lingering Signs of Drought" (#47)

Sarasvati: "Distraction," "Like Primitives," "You Say I Am,"
    "Your Father's Fear"
Venture: "Yanked"

"The Clock Tower" and "Mother and Daughter"
    in *Soaring without Limits: Healing through the Arts* (published
    by Brain Injury Association of Massachusetts and Brockton High
    School).

"Encounter" won a Barbara Bradley Honorable Mention Award, and
"The Speckled Hawk" won a Daniel Varoujan Honorable Mention
Award, with the New England Poetry Club.

In Appreciation

A salute to the teachers and editors who assisted with the formation and revision of these poems: Kim Bridgford of *Mezzo Cammin* and director of Poetry by the Sea, the conference dedicated to all things poetry that gathers us together and sustains us; Timothy Steele and his visionary workshops; Jennifer Barber, director of the Poetry Center at Suffolk University and editor of *Salamander*; to X. J. Kennedy, whose workshop doused early versions of some of these poems with ice water; Doug Holder, Harris Gardner, and Gloria Mindock, of *Ibbetson Street Magazine* and the First and Last Word Poetry Series at the Arts at the Armory in Somerville, Massachusetts; Karen Hafner and the open mike series at Rockland Library; Philip Hasouris and the series at Brockton Public Library; Alice Kociemba and the reading series at West Falmouth Library; Ted Richer and his forums at Quincy College, Umass/Boston, and Bridgewater State University; Jack Scully and the Poetry Series in Plymouth. All of these venues provide attentive and congenial audiences to test poems-in-progress. Thanks to the New England Poetry Club, whose events at the Yenching Library and on the lawn at Longfellow House continue the long tradition of celebrating poetry, and its president emeritus Diana Der Hovanessian, in her memory, with whom one could always take friendship and receive wisdom. To all those who contribute to *The Poetry Porch* and *Sonnet Scroll*! To the members of the poetry discussion group that meets once a month at the Scituate Town Library where we sharpen our wits. To my colleagues and friends whose critiques really help: George Kalogeris, Richard Fein, Marcia Karp, Robert K. Johnson, David Ferry, Lloyd Schwartz, and the late Julia Budenz who first encouraged me to write sonnets. To Sally Davenport for the final edit. Gratitude to my husband John who gives me the time and space to work, and to our daughter Kaelen, whose independence and work ethic, ever brilliant, is a marvel to us all.

Contents

With My Mother-in-Law

Cairo Scenes, 1989

Cairo Seen Again, 2014

Invocation: Sonnets for Sunflowers

May sonnets I create today vibrate
And methods I employ be multiple
Like these self-seeded favorites of Van Gogh
Who stand together, many eight feet tall.

May several lines exact their bright appeal
As blossoms do in hues of gold and yellow,
Whose crenellated crowns of petal silk
Surround a fertile darkness at the center.

May stanzas open branches up to let
The songbirds come and feast among the leaves,
Upright or hanging upside down, to rip
And scatter hope by sowing next year's seeds.

Before the blossoms shrink and lose their color,
May these few words record my love of summer.

My Mother and the Rugosa

The rose would die if she were wrong,
Clipping short a thousand lives.
She held the tool's unsharpened knives
And hummed an old familiar song

Whose lyrics helped to quell her fears.
Just as she thought these doubts had fled,
A newborn sparrow raised its head
Between the crossbars of the shears

Beseeching her to end the storm
Of loosened leaves and hacking swords,
To back the promise of her words
With something good, perhaps a worm.

Zinnias and Marigolds in a Porcelain Vase,
by Hermann Dudley Murphy

What companion would you select
In this common country garden?
Both zinnia and marigold,
The elegant and sovereign.

Elegant: The zinnia
Is tall, hard-working, vigorous,
In yellow, pink, magenta splendor,
A favorite of the local vendor
Who praises its unerring charm,
Waltzing on late summer's arm,
Bowing, sumptuous, twirling, chaste,
Beside the rose, almost straight-laced,
Reaching out to gather in;
When cut, its blossoms come again.

Sovereign: The marigold
Will keep its yellow petals rolled;
The double gold anemone
Supports our summer's currency
That must not be withheld but spent
According to our agreement
On what we need, how much we have;
Its beauty, bold and curative,
Can keep the pests away from those
Most precious of our tomatoes.

Where She Was Going

My mother taught me where to find tadpoles in the spring,
To let soup cool in the spoon, and to tie shoe laces twice.

She taught me to scan the headlines for the latest news
And to budget my first allowance when I was twelve.

She would not take me to church. She would not cut my hair.
She would encourage me to monitor my secrets.

I vacuumed my own room, which made her sit and laugh.
She marveled that she didn't know where I was going.

I followed her down the walk that often needed weeding.
With my sister in tow, she pushed me to go first.

Soon I designed my clothes from colorful lengths of cloth.
She praised my work but sighed about the money spent.

She liked to resurrect and use forgotten tools
And swore the old push mower was good for exercise.

Depressions in dirt roads have been filled in and paved.
Now frogs retreat into the woods to lay their eggs.

We peel potatoes, listening to the evening news.
We compose and rewrite a letter to the editor.

We transcribe recipes from hastily written notes.
And soon, if she will let me, I will cut her hair.

I often say that she should follow me, which makes
Her smile. She will not tell me where she is going.

My Last Visit

This driving rain! It only pleases me
Because it brings me to another day
A year ago: I traveled through the cold
On such a day and visited my mother.

I wore the same coat that I wear today,
But then I tugged this hat and wrapped this scarf
To keep the cold, the wet, the weather out.
Today I need to keep my sadness in.

The cold last year was as it is today.
I pulled my suitcase through the drilling rain,
Held my umbrella high against the wind,
And rode the escalator down and down

And out alone. I had come for a reason
And for a privileged moment I forgot—
Oh, yes. She called us all and drew us near,
Who did not know this spring would be her last.

I saw her waiting for me in her car,
Magenta shirt and bright white hair cut short,
Unmistakable on that gray day
Among the cars in that commuter lot.

My mother waited for me under glass
For less than half an hour, shielded from
This life and weather. I still see her as
She waits, a rare protected hothouse flower.

Take and Receive

She gives, I take
The silver cup, the woolen scarf,
Vanilla cream, the old ice skates.

She gives, and I refuse
The curdled eggs, the scalded milk,
The reprimand, the awful shoes.

She gives, to one already full,
Who loves the summer and the snow,
Who mimes the art of letting go.

I take, then I receive
The cup engraved, the scarf resewn,
The courage to achieve,

The tonic against grief,
The habit of delight.

Lingering Signs of Drought

The white root probed late summer underground,
Sought in moist tubers of swelled potatoes

A darkness that encouraged them to take
Their fill, stretch out, and die. At harvest, I

Pulled pliant threads with pincer thumb and nail
Out through the tubers' eyes, and saw, wound tight

Like scrolls preserving written signs, their tongues,
Now hardened lines that held the key to tell

The story of all that had happened when,
With no tomatoes on the vine, no squash,

No gourds, just awful water shortages,
The season ended tasteless, odorless.

Encounter

When I drew near him huddled in the grass
One fine spring day—and what a day it was!—
He asked me if I knew what he possessed.
I stared, insisting that he let me pass.

"I bought this BB gun today," he hissed
As if I had no notion what it was.
He said the land was his, that I trespassed.
I turned to walk away, so soon dismissed.

I left him in the drying peppergrass.
He did not own this land. It was not his.
My vision blurred as through a milky glass.
The tears that fell were hard, as hard as brass.

Encounter with His Brother

I met him on the empty cattle walk.
We knew that he had planned to go away.
I was surprised when he began to talk
To me with sorrow that he could not stay,

That he was going to Jerusalem
Where he would live and work a kibbutz
And learn from people who would counsel him
To match religion with his politics.

Blue clouds assembled like cathedral domes.
The field would give a church its cornerstone,
The farm a plot for tracts of showy homes,
And soon it would be hard to walk alone.

Blueberries

To see them is to covet them:
The tiny ones on small bushes,
The fattened ones on high bushes,
Those in a box filled to the brim.

Unpolished gems of sweet water,
These memories of August sun
Will purple up the mouth and tongue
From now until mid-September.

Tomatoes in September

Each will be delicious in its own way.

Tomatoes on the counter ripening
In window sun are aging differently
As each will slowly turn from green to red.

A sudden score of orange stripes around
One flattened globe grows like the pantaloons
Of someone's family heirloom harlequin.

Another blushes from chartreuse to peach,
As if the changes that originate
From deep within need time for perfection.

The third favors the east over the west,
Producing a lop-sided red effect
Until time's rescue makes the hue complete.

In its own way, each will be delicious.

Poisonous Fruit

"The treatment is like dying every day,"
She said. "And with the cancer cells impaired,
Attacks the healthy ones not far away."
I saw his ravaged body and despaired.

We sliced tomatoes, once thought to be Eve's
Forbidden fruit. The crescents on a plate
With olive oil and snips of basil leaves
Would work, I prayed, to pique his appetite.

My sister joked about the colonists
Who thought that those who ate tomatoes died
Because the unripe fruit was poisonous.
"My body's full of poison," he replied.

He laughed aloud as we tried not to cry.
In silence we addressed our own sorrows.
Then he said, a twinkle in his eye,
"Let's have some more of those ripe tomatoes."

Driving through Amish Country

The narrow Pennsylvania road disclosed
A hooded wagon drawn behind a horse,
A sight as energetic and composed
As by another century endorsed.

We strained to see the handsome bearded man
Who let the reins swing loosely as he sat
Inside the shelter of the hooded van,
His visage framed beneath his broad-brimmed hat.

"This horse can *trot* at speed to match our car!"
My husband emphasized the action verb.
He shifted back, reducing engine power,
Determined not to frighten nor disturb

The concentration of the sprightly bay.
We marveled at the even ticking reel
That held our minds so freely in its sway
As if beneath a universal spell.

We fell to dreaming, free to contemplate
The steady heartbeat as it lulled the mind.
What better measure to decide our fate
Than principles of order it defined?

But soon our four-stroke engine would betray
How by a love of commerce it was made
When our exhaust ejected carbon spray
Against the sanctuary of the glade.

My husband sighed, his patience nearly burst.
"Time for a tune-up," he said, in a funk.
And suddenly it seemed that we were cursed,
Transporting poison hidden in the trunk.

The pattern in the rhythmic tapping groove
Continued as the buggy headed south.
We watched the horse, I studied every move,
And then we turned to take the highway north.

The Speckled Hawk

Now we suspect the speckled hawk has been
Here many times, the reason anxious crows
And jays intensify their cries, and spin
For no apparent cause, until she shows

Her profile from her perch. There, pressed in flat
Against the trunk, she hides in spotted light.
She looks across her shoulder at the fat
Contented hens below, soon bunched in tight.

Now I can count how frequently she came,
Recalling where two chickens in the snow
Had died at separate times yet with the same
Delivery of force, from high to low.

The one who gashed and opened up the breast,
Consumed the innards, scooping out the heart—
And left the head, and wings and feet, the rest
To rot—fulfilled her designated part.

Today I listen for her quiet climb.
She turns and drops down close as if she would
Negotiate—but no, she needs no time
To map the layout of our neighborhood.

I cannot say her actions have outweighed
Distortions of her predatory nature;
Aloft, borne on the arrow she has made,
She strikes to live and does not pause to torture,

And does not wish but takes, without an argument,
As long ago, she proved the world was hers.
Her pinions weave through each impediment—
The outstretched oaks, the prickly firs—

And gather severed shreds, from strife to strife,
That might explain divisions in her ways—
The softest down, the sharpest knife,
The fierceness in the cry that she betrays.

I Freed a Dove Today

Confused, she spent the night inside our shed.
Perched on a barrel rim and teetering,
She flapped to see me there, my entering
A sight that must have filled her heart with dread.
Not trusting my extended pair of hands,
She flew up to the windowpane and clung
Against the image of the world she'd sung
About before, its pleasures and demands.
The scene beyond the window stayed in view.
I improvised a perch of pole and head
Without its stringy mop, and then, with daft
Finesse, I held it up. She stepped, I led.
She saw that she could ride on this lone shaft—
And there it was! The World! And there she flew!

Late Spring at Sixty

The bees cannot wake themselves up this year;
Excess pollen coats the puddles and rims.

When the rain comes, I hear a sudden hiss,
The sound of drops breathing. Or do they break?

Apple blossoms float to the ground and scatter;
My verse forms are studded with tiny seeds.

When I come in from the garden, I shed
Sand and grit like diamonds on the pages.

Nature no longer wants to flirt with me.
Jilted, I nurse new allergies at night.

Before I work outside, I shower to
Cleanse my body in homage to the earth.

Although I still adore the sun, I will
Create my tan carefully from a jar.

I ingest bacteria with each breath,
The aftertaste of unseen enemies.

A fondness compels me to move these rows
Of seedlings in line with the morning sun.

Where my husband has worked to turn the soil,
Dandelions celebrate their good luck.

The asparagus rises, first a stalk,
Then a wild spray of green exuberance.

The grackle sits at the feeder and gobbles
Throatfuls of grain, with one eye fixed on me.

You Say I Am

A sequence of poems
For John

The Envy of the Gods

Because we feared the envy of the gods
We hid the love we felt. We strived, inspired
By days and weeks of breaking up old sods
To live like farmers, overworked and tired.

We bought a house that no one else would want.
Aware our cash would never add a speck
To books that measure wealth, we did not taunt
Our luck but cashed and hoarded every check.

We filled our plot with modest herbs and greens.
Beneath the burning sun, the falling star,
We spat on passion, acted out in scenes
To trick the gods observing from afar

So they might praise what we had undertaken:
A quiet life, hardworking and soft-spoken.

In Times of Emergency

Once the wars overseas had ended, we
Expected an immediate release;
Instead it seemed impatience turned the key
That kept us from achieving inner peace.

This afternoon, while holding off the flu
I push this pen, precipitate a fight
As inside would what outside does not do,
Dismantle all we've earned and travel light.

Some say external threats of war and strife
Induce the need for love, and that the fears
Of uneventful days at home, the empty life,
Drive those apart who vowed to stay for years.

We hold each other close where stairs descend
And when we sense the wars will never end.

Your Coat

In memory of Pat Fiandaca

To make your coat, I studied with a man
From Italy, with years behind his trade,
Who held the rule but measured by the span
Of what he knew from all the things he made.

With gentleness, he humored my ambition
And softened my mistakes with gentle talk.
We shaped lapels according to tradition:
Stitching, steaming, marking up with chalk.

"This coat is finer than a lion's pelt,"
He said. A pelt with stripes, from black to tan?
He joked that we could always add a belt.
Finished at last, he praised: "Here is a man!

"This coat is for the man of modest wealth.
May he live long and wear it in good health."

Like Primitives

Like primitives, who must arise and drive
Through mornings cruel and seasons cavalier,
We summon Gods when we feel most alive
And hate it when they seem to interfere.

At dawn you leave before the experts know
The weather, type of clouds, or hue of day,
And go to work with lofty dreams in tow
Until you reach your office on the bay.

You stash your dreams behind the cabinet door
That closes like a rock across a cave,
Reverberating in the mind of Thor
Who would release us on an ocean wave—

Instead, each night he bludgeons us to sleep
Till mechanistic birds explode and bleep.

Distraction

I love you to distraction—
Distracted, find the key
To penetrate the kingdom
And live beneath the sea.

Your crab-like form approaches
My shoulder, from the side—
With eyes like tiny lanterns
Glowing in the tide.

The shadow near an ice floe
Becomes a polar bear—
Ingesting salty water
And belching fragrant air.

Although the currents tumble
And phosphoresce in rains
Immersing us in silver—
Our appetite remains.

Your Father's Fear

You ladle out
Your father's fear
In golden beer
And sable stout.

With honeyed rum
From local bees
And Pekoe teas
Our mothers hum.

We puzzle thoughts
In tangled skeins
Of ceiling stains
And oaken knots.

Another quaff
And we are off.

You Say I Am

You say I am your premier motivator
And I say you are just a putter-upper,
Who wears the same old coat throughout the year
And shrugs about the stormy front that's near;
Who uses cast-off string to tie his shoes,
And pockets change, and hates to have to choose
Between arrays of coffee, white to black,
And if it's sweetened, wants his money back;
Who rides a motorcycle off to work
With heated vest and gloves, a novel quirk;
Who once decided not to ever shave
Until the winter crawled back in its cave;
Who says it doesn't matter if we're late;
So, as I check my watch, we smile and wait.

Contriving Blue

At first, we loved, two grouse engrossed
With no more thought than one for two
And spent our days like lovers soused
Imbibing and contriving blue.

What I had known you understood:
We loved, as first we had been loved
According to our family's mood,
Our mothers pulled, our fathers shoved.

Yet what I am I keep with you
Captive in this primrose frame,
And what you are is lost in blue
Although you claim to be the same.

He Would Not Stay

Our cat would not stay at our new address.
New carpeting was foul to him, the shiver
Of bright lamps too strange. Far from the river
Now, he missed the routine restlessness

And we missed it too, how we missed the way
We lived our lives there, above the noise
And dogs, the Friday nights that vagrant boys
Got drunk and cursed our nascent dreams away,

Dreams that in the new place we'd have to hone
And shape and polish, work much harder at,
Enough to shake up our big sleepy cat,
Who walked the distances back home alone

To conquer space, and trade, with every climb,
The present for the past to conquer time.

If I Should Leave You

If I should leave you, everyone will know
How strong these terrors run beneath the ices;
The sullen spirits that our faces show
Will seem a symptom of our needs and vices.

If we should make a north-from-south divide
And stake our reputation on our fences,
We'll soon unleash the monsters we denied
And curse the need to pay back all expenses.

We hail the worst in each, in each condone
The remedy for pain; we know our faults.
What use will parting bring to one alone?
We'll have to lock our hearts in separate vaults.

If you should leave me, we will be at war,
When peace is what we say we're fighting for.

For the Love of a Book

1.

Librarians suspect a thief.
The book I seek I know by heart,
Its fragile shape, vanilla leaf,
Well-seasoned script, old-fashioned art,

Whose author knows how much I crave
Its words—O printed cellulose!—
Which ripen slowly on the page
And tantalize the eyes and nose

And fill the cauldron of the mind
With figments rising into speech
In revelations of the kind
That otherwise seem out of reach.

2.

The sentries at the reference desk
Hold back a watchdog's throaty growl,
Regard me through their granny specs,
And make a mark inside their file.

Those who keep volumes under glass
Can neither share the eloquence
Of newsprint rendered in its sauce,
Nor bindings' tasty succulence,

Nor enter into dialogue
With gusto of a connoisseur
By scratching in the margin's edge
And adding salt to signature.

3.

This book, it's true, I loved to pieces,
Have known, as it is known about.
Behold, despite the nicks and creases,
That no one cut the pictures out.

And so I ask you to relent
Before my hunger, now discerned.
The book I chose was hardly spent,
But tasted, savored, and returned

To each, its designated case,
Where wealth and poverty collide
Within the bounty of this place
That leaner worlds cannot provide.

A Community Gathered

in response to the Fire Alarm at the Poetry Conference,
6:00 a.m.

The siren would have made Poseidon reel!
Like Gods they rose in groggy dishabille:
First Hermes staggered through without a robe,
Enfeebled by the lamp's fluorescent strobe,

While Aphrodite, wrapped in pink peignoir,
Left the heavy exit door ajar,
And Hestia joked that she'd sneak unawares
To meet the mighty Ares on the stairs,

As Demeter, in crisis with a frown,
Tried to fix her hair, half up, half down,
While Hera, wearing ugly cotton pants,
Cursed her husband Zeus in sibilants.

As if he thought he soon might be betrothed,
Apollo rushed outside completely clothed.

Wingèd Creature

The night had raised an early summer storm,
And then the morning sent me fluttering.
Your garden stones, inviting and so warm,
Attracted me, for I was shivering.

You watched me in contortions of distress
And picked me up and held me in your palm;
And then the ardor of your sudden kiss
Enveloped me with passion and alarm.

I might have stayed a month, or even more
Where waters shimmered, artfully controlled
Between embankment flora fed with ore.
And then *my* veins were pumped with liquid gold.

I laughed at you and shouldn't have, transfixed
By this moment. I was the woman charmed.
But once I found my wings, these pinions flexed.
You stooped to catch your love. I flew transformed.

Unemployed

Some inspirations find themselves in song,
And blest are they who keep the message short;
Thus, I assure you I won't take too long
To compensate for being out of work.

For what is work beyond a single goal
That someone else imposes on your mind,
That ties you to your worst supporting role,
And counsels you to leave the best behind?

It is my hope that morning's mood improves
By afternoon, and winter's rare delight—
The crimson clouds that evening's wind removes—
Will bring Orion's stars into the night.

This poem marks the movements of the day
I gathered in my wealth, to give away.

Yanked

On the Red Line, from Harvard Square to Park Street

Notes from the vibraphone recount
Water from a choppy fount.
While prancing in a bluesy ring
The saxophonist's gait has swing.

We board the train and head downtown
To rattle through the underground,
Like circles caught in squares of plaid
Or blind percussionists gone mad.

And then we reach the narrow bridge
Above the river. As it flows,
We stop and look over the edge.

The engine yanks us on our way,
And we long for the sounds of those
Two jazz musicians, who could play!

Opening a Book of Poems by Michael Drayton
and Finding Pages Uncut

The introduction made excuses for effect.
In publishing this book, it hung, an albatross,
Around the printer's neck, while bringing on the loss
Of the first editor, who died at mid-project.
I turned the heavy pages, hard-shelled like a nut,
But in the printed sequence found that some were hidden
By a self-made envelope, as if forbidden:
Folded, stitched, and bound, but not yet scored nor cut.
It seemed a failure or confusion that implied
A book was made that would withhold what lay inside.
Still, it reminded me that readers with a knife
Can open up a book as well as take a life.
I sat to read and comprehend another age
From long ago, when ink like blood infused the page.

Two Temperaments

For Julia Budenz

One rises from the bottom and explodes
In revelations sparkling on the surface;
The other sinks in basins of the cosmos
To steep and ruminate the ancient codes.
How good it is to choose contemporaries
And spend the hour articulating phrases
Under the aegis of centuries of sages
Refined in labyrinthine-halled libraries.
If time should prove these conversations wasted,
O let each be served with sugar or with lemon
In cups or ladles, cisterns of the czars!
Let no one deprecate these trends we tasted
As we compare the Greek verse with the Roman
Or reconstruct those years between the wars.

Carpentry

In Memory of Seamus Heaney

O come and see the bookcase he has made
Where light beneath the lantern's linen blind
On timbers salvaged by the sawyer's blade
Illuminates the seams, the staves aligned,

Where uprights plumb against the wall and eaves
Become the chariot on which he goes
Across the waves and shifting vellum leaves
That bear his words and what it is he knows,

To navigate the best of times and worst,
To teach us how to read the lines and measure
Works of those who voiced their visions first.
We did not see the ferry floating closer.

Directing our attention, he called, Aye!
With nods and smiles, and we watched him go over
To the place beyond, where he'd abide
With father, mother, and his little brother.

The lapping of the waves against the crooks
Of logs will trace the time, though time may lag,
And then the raft become a wall of books
With mitred shelves that hold and do not sag.

The White Cat

Alone in the upholstered chair,
I settle in to write.
He seeks my face, as if to say,
This is no time to work.

I'm making art, I clarify.
Not work but play, he adds.
He practices a silent leap,
I trace a verbal arc.

He sets himself apart and stares
At patterns in the plaster;
I turn and watch the single page
Where surface letters scatter.

He waits for an emerging mouse,
I for emerging thought;
His onyx pupils shrink and swell,
My pencil swoops and falls.

We spend the morning hours thus,
Shedding lead and hair;
Today I fail to find the words,
Today he sleeps too much.

He's happiest when he can hold
His prize beneath his claws;
My gladness comes with insight plucked
From knots in ancient laws.

He sits, a bookend propped against
The shadows as they fade;
I fill my pen again with ink
And darken up the page.

Between the evening and the day,
We tally up our work.
He sets his quarry on the hearth;
I weigh the words I wrote.

The Fledgling

1

Our mother put the fat baby bird
on a litter of grass and leaves
at the bottom of a makeshift cardboard crib.

It stood up and wobbled
on nearly useless legs and flattened claws,
its head thrown back;

beady eyes set in a gray nimbus of fluff;
wings arrayed like unfinished
folded fans;

its yellow beak closed in a grimace,
opened into a small round cavern,
triangular tongue across the gullet.

We used tweezers to set bits of bread,
watermelon, a dead fly deep in its throat,
the way its mother might have.

It roused its tiny tiger self
and spoke. I am!
Soon the whole crate shook with its attempts to fly.

2

A Mocker!
proclaimed the young receptionist,
a volunteer ornithologist,

who recognized at once
the gray and white songbird it would become
if nurtured in its proper kingdom.

She showed us the heated cage
where it would grow
with others of its species,

for, though we rescued it from harm
and meant the best by it, she said
we had not given it a proper diet.

And when we caught her eye again
she asked if we would leave a small donation,
fifteen dollars minimum.

3

The car was empty as we drove away
from the suburban sanctuary.
How we missed those piercing baby cries!

At home, our mother could not quell her rage,
having left the baby bird—with an "expert"—
in that awful heated cage.

Her Tattoo

A conversation piece, it draws in strangers
      at parties, on the subway.
She tells them sweetly where she had it done,
      how much it didn't hurt,
what it cost.

This perennial blue wreath of flowers
      around her ankle like an amulet
makes her the envy of her peers,
      who praise the artist's handiwork,
petals and garlands without roots

etched like a scar into the surface
      of her flesh, as if to announce, "There will be
no dialogue; this is the person
      I am becoming. Regard the adorn-
ment of my pain."

               ***

We went to New Hampshire, where it's legal;
      August 1992, my sixteenth year,
$80.00 (it was not your money).
      Tracy drove; it was her idea,
then she chickened out.

***

Beneath the ornate exterior
       a message to me? A sign like
a change of name or address,
       does it put me in my place:
a mother discharged?

All this in my face, daring me to express disgust.
       I say I'll pay the bill if she
ever decides she wants a skin graft.

She Regards Michelangelo's Piéta at St. Peter's Cathedral

Our daughter studied modern art in class
With someone who, or so the rumor said,
Had shared Picasso's studio and bed
And might defend the placement of the glass

Before the pair, so chaste and isolate.
We waited till the noisy crowds dispersed
To view the son as if at peace in sleep,
His mother's face in peace inviolate.

The bodies, yes, the bodies worked their spell:
The man's, whose beauty taught us what it meant
To be a man and to be loved, as if
We might forget and, misadvised, rebel.

If he stood up, our daughter slowly spoke,
His sculpted head would reach a height so great
That he'd exceed the limits of this cell,
The comfort of his mother's arms and cloak.

We marveled, I at truth in lowly facts,
She at muscled limbs, athletes, and myth.
Did she see God, or godlike man adrift?
Divinity, or man's destructive acts?

I stammered with advice on monuments,
The qualities of stone, God's love and wrath,
On loving men who love you back, who leave,
Who take, who topple trees and battlements,

The man you see when death reveals his length,
The man of your own size, who is not tall.
She did not tell me further what she saw
But fixed upon a mother's love, full strength.

Commencement

She graduates triumphant, proud to win.
We crane our necks and snap her photograph,
And here I want to emphasize *begin,*
Although the day is at its end. We laugh.

We laugh as though, through simple force of will,
She might escape the lessons her fate,
As if, because of years she spent at school,
All future tragedies will have to wait.

I swallow sorrow as I scan the sky
And memorize the day as in a book,
Admitting that I see a sweet good-bye
Recorded in the photos that we took.

Mother and Daughter

from a Black and White Photograph

We dressed in white theatrical and fine
Like patients signed with Doctor Frankenstein.

I whispered, pressing lips against her hair,
Would she agree that we were quite a pair?

My voice was soft, my feelings chafed and raw.
She laughed as if we shared the thing we saw:

My illness that would give us both a poke.
It takes a pair to make a private joke,

A pair that shares the bones and blood and genes
For days and years, matching up the scenes,

Until electric currents take control.
The spike erased the lion of my soul.

My illness grew and changed the house around.
We fought; she lost the center ground.

While I retreated, mannered as a mouse
To melt through the all borders of the house,

She lost her bid to play the role of host,
The very time I needed her the most.

With Three Graces

Aglaia   *Brilliance*
Euphrosyne *Joy*
Thalia   *Bloom of Life*

Aglaia:

Community of blossoms in a vase.
Ceremonial ribbon, tied and bowed.
The helianthus nodding to amaze
The blue-eyed grass that morning workers mowed.

Euphrosyne:

The buttercup of the ranunculus
Will bounce its hue from petals held to chin.
Recall how as a child that delighted us?
Now with a child, begin this game again.

Mother:

Or take this colorful geranium:
With petals like the neck and bill of cranes,
A bird-like dolphin, from delphin, means womb
In Greek. The roots combine and take the names.

Daughter:

The roots define, the names connect the roots.
Oh sit down mother, twine your amulets
With flora of your own garden, the shoots
You have arranged of vinca, violets.

Mother:

Like honeysuckle, vines embrace
The flowering oregano and thyme,
The basils, mints, and Bergamot, with peach,
And cherry, apple, almond, pear, and lime—

Daughter:

If only they all bloomed at once, today!
But they must bloom in their own time and way.
Here, hold the baby, let me show you how
She likes to lie, for I'm the expert now.

Thalia:

The baby who smiles will bring her family joy:
See how her darling infant lips unfurl,
A blossom opening for all the world.

The Clock Tower

This painting of a village I would keep
Where streets are straight and distant mountains steep.
The handsome clock high on the red-roofed tower
Controls the bells that mark each quarter hour.

The mural on the wall beneath the clock
Depicts the Shepherd leaning to his flock,
Teaching them that in his care they're safe,
But, once, I was convinced the bells were late:

A funeral mass was winding through the town,
Its windows shuttered and its awnings down.
I dreamed that all my friends had come to see
The candles and the service, held for me,

But no one spoke my name or knew my case.
I saw the clock had lost its hands and face.
Without the time, how could I hope to tell
The many ways I stumbled, tripped, and fell?

I know this place. It's not so far away,
A quiet town where quiet people stay,
Where accidents and injuries are real,
Where I could learn to suffer and to heal.

Elegy

He felt his strength failing, and so, came home.
The doctor brought the newest medicine;
His mother learned to handle a syringe.
In weeks, he wasted down to skin and bone.
Afraid his mind was causing him to ramble,
He read up on the news so he could charm
The visitors who came filled with alarm
About the way he looked. "It's such a shamble,"

He would say about the featured crimes
And beam his sunny smile on those inclined
To press him with regret or deep remorse.
He combed his hair and flirted with the nurse.
The youngest, always running from behind,
He died in bed on Sunday with the *Times*.

Still the Same

We drove right home from the airport,
Opened the door to our house where

The sunlight pouring through windows,
Geranium above the sink,

Enameled table with papers,
Old maps, and books were all the same.

Outside, the gardens were the same,
The grass still green, the maple red,

The yellow marigolds still full,
The zinnias still red, orange,

Magenta, lemon, pink, and white.
I saw the signs of early frost:

The withered leaves down near the ground,
The browned petals on several blooms

Above. But most were still so bright
And full: they seemed the same. I clipped

Them for the blue ceramic vase,
Brought apples up from the cellar

To make a cake. A cake in the oven
Would warm up the chilly kitchen.

Soon we would go and get your mother
And bring her home from the hospital.

How glad she would be to see the kitchen
With apples ready for a cake,

The sunlight pouring through windows,
Geranium above the sink,

Enameled table with papers,
Old maps, and books, the woolen hat.

How she would smile at flowers still
Colorful in the bright blue vase.

If skies should turn and winds flatten
The green grass, then tear the burnt leaves

From the branches of the red maple—
If rain should fall with pelting sounds—

We would sit together, waiting
For the cake to rise, to taste it, to

Agree it was as good as one
We baked before, the special one

We remembered, when all that we
Knew seemed to rise up from our share

Where it was still, and our love the same.

With My Mother-in-Law

Studying Arabic

I like to write the alphabet
In looping movements right to left,
Which suits my own left-handedness
Accustomed to the counter turn
Expected of the clockwise scripts.

She did not learn the language by
Writing but memorized the lessons
From her mother, who taught her words
To utter in familial sounds
That would always keep them together.

I like the way the word for friend
Lines up the letters on the page
And tongue. *"Habibe,"* she laughs, "The word
For my dear one, and our nickname
For our father, when we were young."

She shakes her head in anger at
Herself when she cannot remember
What was once so familiar.
I struggle with the awkward forms
Beneath my pencil and eraser.

Engaged with our respective tasks,
We stretch the paradigms foretold
And reaffirm the promises:
What was empty now is full;
What was idle now betrothed.

Family Talk

She shut her eyes against the bright surroundings.
Sensing the time was right, I said I'd like
To move the dining room mahogany—
"Oh no," she said, "No changes when I'm down!"

They wheeled her to another room where she
Was scheduled for a facial MRI.
She brought her hands up to her cheeks and joked,
"I'd planned to get another facial soon."

We had a chance to talk, the first in weeks.
She asked, "Were you aware how mad he was?"
She meant her son, my husband, who, I said,
Was getting like his father, impatient Scot.

She disagreed. "Oh no, not HIS father,"
She emphasized, "but like MY father!"
I recognized her anger down so deep—
There's nothing like the Middle East for rage.

The nurse came in to stitch the several cuts
Where she had fallen forward on her face.
"I don't know how much longer I will last,"
She said, and grabbed my hand, and held it fast.

Kitchen Clean-up

Her history was stored in that cupboard:
Glasses, cups, and measurers were stacked
And grouped in triple rows too densely packed
For use, unless for an entire horde

Of kids and college kids and grownup kids.
Look at this ornamented pewter stein
Designed as if it's from an ancient time
When tankards were so big, and came with lids.

The pair of pastel tumblers perfect for
Pink lemonade, a picnic, once a year;
And look, your brother's high school souvenir.
What has she kept them all together for

Beside the nested plastic sippy cups,
In case the little ones might come to play?
We put these keepsakes carefully away
Inside a bag to make space for the grownups,

A phrase that made her smile and bite her lip.
The grownup of the grownups, she was grown.
She held her favorite glass. "This is my own,"
She winked, "until I make my final trip."

Her Passing

Your mother's death at 3:30 a.m.,
The quiet hour saved for births and deaths,
Came as she would have wanted it.

I'm glad I was awake when the call came
And I could tell you of the nurse's plea
To hurry to your mother's side.

I'm glad I was the one who chose her clothes,
the handkerchief embroidered with her name,
The silk chemise, the tailored blouse.

I'm glad I was the one who sang the songs,
Recited verses, stood and took the host,
And heard your brother speak his mind.

I'm glad I was prepared to find the gifts—
The call, the clothes, the ritual, the host—
That she arranged and left for me.

I'm glad I was the one to hear the news
About her spirit's thrashing and escape,
And not her roommate, who was deaf.

I'm glad I was awake to know the hour
Of her quick transformation into fire
And its admission into us.

Song: My Home of Long Ago

Old friends no longer send us cards, their whereabouts unknown.
I wonder if the tree I climbed is sorely overgrown.
The time has come, I'm going back, to see if what I know
Will help me find my place again, my home of long ago.

With every state I drive across, I fear a little more.
What If I meet my mother's face, awaiting at the door?
O how I long to find her there, to smile and say hello,
And say it's just the way it was, my home of long ago.

> I worry that the place I left will sink and disappear,
> My childhood but a memory, more distant every year.

But someone new is on the porch to meet me at the drive.
A mother and her little girl approach as I arrive.
They welcome me, and make me tea, and show me how they go
To make this house the one they love, this home of long ago.

I praise the changes that have come where everything is new;
The kitchen and appliances, the window with a view,
My father's grace, a glowing trace, in sunlight bending low.
They thank me for the gift we made, our home of long ago,
> Our home of long ago.

Cairo Scenes, 1989

Detour

Returning from the Valley of the Kings,
We took the air-conditioned tourist bus
Away from the security and chaos
Of designated roads. It lurched and stopped.
The driver closed his eyes and seemed to shake.
What was it we were not supposed to see?
The camels waiting for their certain deaths?
A merchant gesturing outside his shed,
Haphazard lean-to—leaning into life—
Where, underneath the desert sun, they say,
No meat will spoil, and so it hangs for sale?
An egg caught in the gullet of a snake
Could work its way through such a narrow sphere
But we seemed paralyzed by our mistake.

Like Emerson

Another bus was squeezing close beside;
Its busy passengers engaged in talk
Had hardly noticed us. Our windows up,
We could not ask them if they knew the way.
A man across from me returned my stare.
In gray wool suit and spectacles, he bore
The patience of a sage, like Emerson
Whose self-reliant wanderer would find
Great solitude amid distracting crowds.
He showed no need to ask why we were there.
Indeed, we could not say why we were there,
A real embarrassment to us, for sure,
And inconvenience now to each of them,
Who could not pass until we gave them room.

At the Citadel

We crossed the threshold of the mosque, allowed
Because the men had all gone home to lunch.
Expecting to be swallowed up, perplexed,
By facts and details of interior effects,
We met instead a space so vast it seemed
To push us out into a sea of emptiness
Rather than draw us in. We shrank to specks.
The light from ceiling chandeliers was dim;
We could not tell what we should understand
And left respecting every pilgrim's need to pray
To come to terms with such enormity
Where carpet covers stone and cushions knees
Beneath a dome whose special atmosphere
Can summon storms and havens for the soul.

On the Terrace

The terrace promised a more human scale
Where men and women did not seem so small.
I held my camera, focusing the lens,
To clarify the shapes of city scape—
A brown, intriguing, treeless neighborhood—
When suddenly a gaggle of young girls
Surrounded me as if I were their prize.
I put the Nikon down and slowly turned
To meet them face to face, or girl to girl,
In blessings of our mutual delight.
I looked at them, they looked at me—
Their patterned scarves, my flowered skirt—in thrall
By virtue of our close proximity
To universal giddiness and awe.

These Cairo Girls

Their teacher, young and male, who spoke English,
Explained that they had traveled with the school
From their district, which I could see beyond
The wall, if I would turn again and look.
It all seemed blank to me, without a map
Or other references that might explain.
With little else to say, we shrugged and smiled.
They turned to go and I to walk away
But not before we made a covenant
To celebrate our differences with one
More careful pause—in which I pledged to see
Them each as they must be themselves, in hope
That they will see me as I am myself—
Unique together in this desert place.

Girl in Blue

Her dress was ankle-length electric blue,
The blue of ancient *lapis lazuli*
Swirling like the layered ocean depths
That roll beneath a blue celestial sky.
The movement in her stride and carriage spoke
Of women now and centuries before
On sand that once refused to be defined
But now was hard, as hard as hammered gold.
I saw, in her, traditions looming large
And freedom in imagined space, that would—
Not just to me, to my subjective eye—
Appeal to all who happened to be out
And walking in this brilliant winter light
Alone through Cairo's early morning street.

Cairo Seen Again, 2014

Building and Rebuilding

No one walks alone in Cairo now.
The streets are silenced under martial law.
Where freedom in the public space emerged
And was raised up, a banner for the world,
Traditions of building and rebuilding
Live, in the makers of the barricades,
The rescuers, dispensers of first aid,
In women now and centuries ahead
Who play their part in unrestricted space
And haul their buckets to the gates to fill,
Who wait, as four regimes have come and gone,
To get on with their lives, not as before
But as they must, to carry water through
The safety zone, and then to carry on.

Google the Girl

Google the girl with the blue bra
And you will find her lying, raw

Forced over, knocked down on her back
Her legs upraised against attack

From fully-clad helmeted men
Who stare down at her abdomen

Yank off her robe, expose her rib
Punch out the helpless man she's with

Then pin her down with boot to throat,
And step away, better to gloat

And judge, assured that she's at fault
Because she suffered the assault

And cannot prove they ever took
Unlawful steps, all by the book.

Privacy of Dreams

Taken from the visions of her dreams
And woven through with filaments of light,
Her garment held the promise of her dreams
Close to her heart, protected from the light.

Her pounding heart defied their pounding boots.
She trusted in the privacy of dreams.
To punish her, they lifted up their boots,
And when they stepped, they trampled on her dreams.

Between Regimes

Was she one of those girls I met that year
On the porch of the massive Citadel?
She'd be nearly forty years old by now,
Much older than the girl in this small screen.
Perhaps her mother was the one I met,
Who must have seen her fall. Perhaps an aunt.
Her sister and her brother must have seen
Her fall, her father must have seen and wept.

What happened to the promise of the spring?
We waited and tomorrow never came.
A weight swings back and forth between regimes,
Each one oppressive, unopposed, and armed,
A different face but with the same decree:
"Whoever is afraid shall stay unharmed."

Evening into Day

And what of others just like her?
Have they arrived at Tahrir Square
While outside, martial law explodes
In clouds of tear gas, isla-mist
As protestors arrange the cars
Between the hutch and hospital
Not far from guards who order tanks
To flatten makeshift camps and tents?

Have others fallen as she fell
But undetected by the press?
Have they been able to get up,
To make their way to solid ground,
Not to proclaim an evening done
But to announce a day begun?

Bluze

Was this one of the girls I knew
Those twenty years ago?

I seek a word in Arabic
For blue and find "azraq"

And blood is "dam" and bird is "tayr"
And swallow is "sununu"

While shirt is qamis, also "bluze."
I would create a garment—

Cut out of woven blue chambray
And stitched into a blouse

To cover up the healing bruise—
And while I sew, I'll sing

An old familiar tune, a blues
To send our fears away—

I'll sing it for myself but I'll
Offer it to her—

The kind of song you can carry
A blues with a feeling

Whether working or out walking
That's what I have today.

Notes

"Your Coat" was inspired by a class in tailoring (1973) that I took with Pasquale (Pat) Fiandaca, Alfred Fiandaca's father, who customized men's suits at the Harvard Cooperative Society for several decades.

"For the Love of a Book" was inspired by the essay "Never Do That to a Book" by Anne Fadiman, which states, "...[J]ust as there is more than one way to love a person, so is there more than one way to love a book" (*Ex Libris,* New York: FSG, 1998, 38).

"The White Cat" is an imaginative rendering of the anonymous Irish poem "Pangur Ban," which I became familiar with when I studied with the Irish poets. See the many other translations and versions by Robin Flower, Eavan Boland, W. H. Auden, Paul Muldoon, Frank O'Connor, and Seamus Heaney.

"The Clock Tower" is based on a painting by Robert Bonia, and "Mother and Daughter" on a photograph by Mary Merritt. These ekphrastic poems were written for an exhibit and poetry reading at Brockton Public Library sponsored by the Brain Injury Association of Massachusetts (April 2016 and 2018). The poems were published in the catalogue *Soaring without Limits: Healing through the Arts*.

"Building and Rebuilding"
The Arab Spring began on December 18, 2010, and precipitated protests and demonstrations, constituting a revolution in many Middle Eastern and North African countries through 2012. The initial incident occurred in Sidi Bouzid, Tunisia, when a street vendor Mohamed Bouazizi set himself on fire in an act of sacrificial self-immolation to protest the mistreatment he suffered under local officials and police. A familiar figure selling fruit and vegetables, and popular to all, he was known for giving produce away to those who could not pay. He had been stripped of his wares (some produce and a scale) and publicly harassed because he lacked a permit to

operate his cart or had not kept up with payment of bribes. After he was taken to an intensive care unit in a Tunisian hospital, he died from his burns on January 4, 2011. The demonstrations that commemorated his death escalated into a series of protests against government mistreatment and corruption across the countries of Algeria, Yemen, Jordan, Saudi Arabia, and Egypt. <en.wikipedia.org/wiki/Mohamed_Bouazizi>

The four regimes is a phrase from Rami G. Khoury, "Anthropology, not politics, rules in Egypt," *The Daily Star*, January 20, 2014. The four—Hosni Mubarak and the National Democratic Party, the Supreme Council of the Armed Forces, the Muslim Brotherhood, and now the current transitional government installed by the armed forces again.

"Between Regimes"
"Do you remember the tomorrow that never came?" Cairo street graffiti quoted by Patrick Cockburn in his review of *Once Upon a Revolution, An Egyptian Story* by Thanassis Cambanis (New York: Simon & Schuster, 2015) which appeared in *The New York Times Book Review,* February 15, 2015, page 19.

"Whoever is afraid stays unharmed," a saying quoted by Wael Ghonim in *Revolution 2.0,* a Memoir. Boston: Houghton Mifflin Harcourt, 2012, page 3.

"Bluze" was inspired by reading N. Awde & K. Smith, *Arabic Practical Dictionary*, New York: Hippocrene Books, Inc., 2004.

About the Author

Joyce Wilson is editor of *The Poetry Porch,* a literary magazine on the Internet since 1997. Wilson's poems have appeared in many literary journals, among them *American Arts Quarterly, Poetry Ireland, Ibbetson Street Magazine,* and *Alabama Literary Review.* Her full-length poetry collection, *The Etymology of Spruce,* and a chapbook, *The Springhouse,* both appeared in 2010. Another chapbook, *The Need for a Bridge* was published in March 2019. Her profiles of the poets Eavan Boland, Julia Budenz, Etel Adnan, and Diana Der Hovanessian (TBA) can be read on the Women Poets Timeline Project at *Mezzo Cammin.* She directs a poetry discussion group once a month at the Scituate Town Library.

Taking classes as a special student at Harvard University for nearly a decade in the 1980s, Wilson received a B.A. through Harvard Extension in 1984 and a M.Ed. from the Graduate School of Education in 1987. During that time she studied writing poetry with Seamus Heaney, writing about poetry with Helen Vendler, in between seminars in English and American literature and education. In 1989, Wilson traveled with her mother and daughter and fifty other Americans to Egypt over the Christmas holidays, a trip that continues to inspire her poems and prose. She worked at Harvard's Woodberry Poetry Room as Assistant to the Curator and Managing Editor of *Harvard Review* from 1992 to 1996 and taught English, at Boston University, and then Suffolk University, for almost two decades.

Wilson and her husband have lived in the same house in Scituate, Massachusetts, on the South Shore of Boston, since 1975. On their acre of land, they grow vegetables and flowers, and raise flocks of chickens, who contribute their eggs and fertilizer to the ongoing process of growing things. They have traveled to Europe and the Middle East several times to catch up with their daughter, a journalist, now married with two daughters, who writes about the arts in Beirut, Lebanon, the locale of her great-grandparents.